REVEALS
The Real Deal
ABOUT
The
Facts
of
(For Boys Only!) # Life

by
Terri Shearer Trenchard

Illustrated by Tracy Councill

Dedicated to
my son, Brady

May you always be empowered
with the gift of knowledge

ACKNOWLEDGEMENTS

This book would have never been born without two very significant people. First, and foremost, there is my husband, George, who nudged me along after my mere mention of writing a children's book. From surrounding me with helpful resources, having more faith in me than I did, and giving me courage to leave behind my consulting gig, he sang my praises and promoted my "book," long before I could even articulate it. George, without you, I would have never begun nor completed this fulfilling journey.

Secondly, I acknowledge my "dear" friend, Sharon Blessing, who (next to my husband) has been my biggest cheerleader, coach, and motivator, from day one. I still remember the moment she looked me in the eye and said, "There's your first book." Whether it was on a regular walk, a daily email, or during one of our weekly "coffees," she inquired about my progress and always provided inspiring, helpful next steps. She began promoting my book long before it was completed. She's already throwing out supporting details for the next book.

The words in my head would have never landed on paper without the enthusiastic support of my mother, Linda McBeth, along with my aunt and uncle (Bev and John Maynard). It was after a ski-break lunch, atop the snow-covered Grand Tetons of Jackon Hole, Wyoming, that their enthusiasm urged me to write the first words upon daybreak the following day. Thank you also to my mother-in-law, Joan Trenchard, whose ongoing inquiry kept me continuing on my task. The interest from all of you made the journey worthwhile.

And, finally, acknowledgement and considerable thanks go to my "reviewers," my treasured friends, colleagues, and family members who read "the book," provided feedback, and offered praises (along with the "Go for it, when can I get one?" wishes). You each provided a valuable perspective and meaningful input. Without you, this would not have kept its momentum. I offer my indebted thanks and appreciation to Kathy Witte, Karen Hennessy, Erika Smith, Margaret Glyder, Meg Whiteford, Dr. Joshua Madden, Jonathan Kahl, Dona Shearer, and my most special pre-teen reviewer: my son, Brady.

I am grateful to each of you for the role you played in the journey of "Bork."

INTRODUCING BORK...
AND THE REAL DEAL

Bork's my name. You heard it right: B—O—R—K. Named after my great, great, great, GREAT-grandfather. Only he didn't have to suffer with a name like Bork. He was Grandione Bork Musgevian, and everyone called him Grand. But not me. No Grand for me. I'm just plain old Bork.

I've heard it all:

Bork the Dork (not funny)

Bork the Snork (even more not funny)

Porky Borky (not funny at all).

That's enough about my name. I'm here to tell you about the real deal on grow-ing up—and about s-e-x. Yep, you read it right: sex.

You gotta be ready. Are you ready?

Okay. Read on.

One of the first things you need to understand is that knowing things gives you power. Knowing things makes you strong. It makes you strong at recess, at lunch, and on the bus. When you know the facts about what your friends are talking about, they respect you. And, you understand what they're talking about. It's cool to know what's going on.

Bork, here, is going to tell you the facts and THE REAL DEAL.

When I talk about THE REAL DEAL, I am talking about...

Puberty

Adolescence

The Facts of Life

I am talking about the changes that happen to all (Did you catch that word?) **all** boys' bodies. I'm also talking about the facts of life (like where babies come from and S-E-X).

Hold on tight.
We'll get to that later.

What exactly are **puberty (pronounced pyoo-ber-tee)** and **adolescence (pronounced ah-duhl-less-sense)?**

Puberty is a stage of growth. Just like other stages of growth. You start out as a baby. Then you are a toddler, followed by a preschooler and an elementary-aged kid. And then you enter puberty and become an adolescent—Yipee Ki Yay, Dude. This is big time stuff.

Puberty usually starts between the ages of 9 and 14. When you are in puberty, it is all about your body changing—in lots of different ways.

Adolescence is a stage of growth after puberty starts. Adolescence usually starts between 11 and 12 and lasts through the late teens and early 20's. You'll hear people talk about puberty and adolescence together. That's because the stages of puberty and adolescence can overlap.

Puberty. Adolescence.

These are big words with big impact.

Say it with me, dude, or just say it in your head: P**yoo-ber**-tee. Don't forget to say the Y. If you say it without the Y (poo-ber-tee), it sounds like you're talking about potty training. We are dealing with something way more important and fascinating.

CAUTION. . .DANGER ! !

Don't read this all by yourself.

Read (at least some parts) with an adult.

Or give it to an adult to read.

Or, if you really have to read it by yourself, be brave and ask questions. Adults know THE SCOOP and they will give you the straight talk. Why? Because they've been there. And, believe it or not, they remember. They were kids. Just like you. Talk to them. They know the scoop.

What?
Do I hear you mumbling?

You think your mom or dad (or another adult) might be uncomfortable talking about this? You think YOU might be uncomfortable talking about this? You may have a point there. But, don't short-change those adults in your life. Mom or dad (or another adult in your life) may be waiting for a chance to talk about this stuff.

But, just in case, allow me (The Grand Bork) to give you some other ideas. You can talk to an older brother, a cousin, an uncle, or another trusted adult. You can even talk to that pediatrician of yours (you know, that doctor designed for us kids).

This is big-time stuff.
Talk it over with a grown-up.
You'll be glad you did.

Now, on with the good stuff...

CHAPTER 1
YOU KNOW YOU'RE IN PUBERTY WHEN...

...you grow taller and stronger and certain parts of your body grow bigger and you get hair in different places and your voice starts to change and...

Let's slow down.

One of the first things to know about puberty is: everybody begins it at a different time.

Yep, everyone gets to the starting gate at different times and everyone finishes at different times. Just like everyone learned to walk, talk, read, and catch a ball at different times. Some boys start the puberty changes when they are 9, and some boys start the changes when they are 14 or 15. One thing's for sure though...you can't skip it. You will definitely go through it.

And you know what? IT'S ALL NORMAL. Let me repeat that: IT'S ALL NORMAL. It can feel like a wild ride, sometimes, but IT'S ALL NORMAL. Guess what else? Girls generally start puberty before boys. Yep, that's right. They usually beat you to the starting gate. (At least this time) ☺.

And now, for your first **REAL DEAL ACTION CHALLENGE**.

I'll wait patiently here to see if you're up to the task. If you are, here it is:

REAL DEAL ACTION CHALLENGE #1

Ask your dad...or your older brother...
or your uncle...or your grandfather:

When did you start growing taller and stronger and
when did your voice start to change?

(This may give you a clue about when you will go
through these changes. This is because boys tend to
take after the males in their dad's families.)

Growth Spurts and Growing Taller

Many guys grow a lot when they start puberty.

Note to Self: You will grow faster during puberty and adolescence than almost any other time in your life.

That means you'll have a growth spurt.

Speaking of "spurt," who came up with that word anyway—spurt? It sounds like we're fountains or something. As you "spurt" up, the bones in your hands and feet may grow first. A growth spurt may be one of the first signs that you are... entering...puberty.

You may also notice that your arms and legs get longer. Are you ready for the really funny part? Your arms and legs may get longer at different times! Just remember: It might *feel* a little awkward when you begin your puberty growth spurt, but it is all normal.

BEWARE.
TAKE CAUTION.

There have been *actual* reports (from *actual* people) that some people *may* trip over their own feet. This is because in the *possible* event that your hands, feet, arms, and legs grow faster than the rest of your body, it can *possibly* make you feel a bit more clumsy than usual. But, fear not, dude. This will all even out. If you don't believe me, look around at all the adults you know. Are any of them tripping over their own feet? No. Just beware that you *might* feel a bit more clumsy as you go through your growth spurt.

Instead of thinking about whether you might trip over your own feet, consider some facts.

The American Medical Association tells us that:
The average boy grows most between the ages of 14-15,
and usually finishes growing around the age of 20,
but sometimes by 16-17.

I know that for some of you, the million dollar question is:

HOW TALL WILL I BE?

I wish I had the answer; because, if I had the answer, I could win a million dollars. That's why it's the million dollar question. Nobody really knows *for sure*, right now, how tall you will be.

The good news is there are some indicators of how tall you *may* be.

REAL DEAL ACTION CHALLENGE #2

There's a formula from the American Medical Association (AMA) to give you an idea of how tall you might be.

Try it, just for fun.

1. Write down the height of both your parents in inches = Mom _____ Dad _____

2. Add 5 inches to your mom's height = _____

3. Add that number (in #2) to your dad's height = _____

4. Take this number (in #3) (which is mom's height plus 5 inches plus dad's height) and divide by 2 = _____ (Bet you never thought division would actually come in handy.)

This number is an estimate of the height you may be.

This is really just for fun.
Don't get too caught up in your estimate.

Remember that the average height for men in the U.S. is 5 feet, 10 inches[1]; some men are much taller than that, and some are shorter. I know lots of men who grew much taller than both their parents!

....
1   American Medical Association. Boys' Guide To Becoming A Teen. San Francisco, CA, 2006.

OR YOU CAN:

Ask your dad...or your older brother...
or your uncle...or your grandfather:

When did you have a growth spurt?

When did you grow the most?

When did you become as tall as you are now?

(Remember, the growth patterns in your dad's family will give you a clue about when and how you will grow.)

Enough math and guesstimating. On to another sign of puberty...

Your Voice Begins To Change

Change?

What exactly do I mean by *change*?

What I mean is your voice will become lower and deeper—like the voice of an older guy. Often, between the ages of 12 and 14, boys' voices will sometimes begin to go up (in a higher, lighter voice) and then down (in a deeper, lower voice). This will sometimes happen in the same sentence! Your voice might be high (and even squeaky) one minute, and then low and deep the next minute. You may actually have two voices that come out for a little while. Freaky, dude.

Hey, you could have fun with this. You can sneak up on your brother or sister and really confuse him or her.

Let me give you a little tip: BE AWARE that you may not know when which voice is about to come out. It could be your BIG DADDY VOICE or the LITTLE KID AROUND THE BLOCK VOICE. Here's another tip: Remember, it is all normal.

When your voice starts to change, you are telling the world out there that you are GROWING UP, without actually shouting: PEOPLE, I'M GROWING UP HERE!! DON'T YA SEE IT??

Your voice may go up, and your voice may go down, but hang loose. Don't let it embarrass you. (You have friends for **that**.) Besides, all you gotta do is look around. Your friends are going through this puberty thing. And all those adults went through the puberty thing. When you think about **the fact** that just about everybody around you is either **going through** it or **went through it**, you gotta figure there's really not much to be embarrassed about.

Guess why your voice goes up and down? It's because your larynx (pronounced **lar**-inks) gets bigger. What the heck is a larynx, you ask. It's your voicebox. It's what makes you talk, sing, hum, yell, and make all those gross sounds that boys our age like to make.

During puberty, your larynx gets bigger and your vocal chords get longer, thicker and wider. As your larynx grows, you also grow a permanent lump in the middle of your throat. Don't panic. This is perfectly normal. It is called your Adam's Apple.

REAL DEAL ACTION CHALLENGE #3
1) Look around at some men.
2) Notice their Adam's Apples.
That's it. Just look around. And notice.

Look around. Notice all the Adam's Apples in older guys and men? See, it's normal. And, when you notice *your* Adam's Apple, you'll know you're in puberty.

By the way, most boys have an Adam's Apple, and girls do not. Why, you ask? Because girls' voice boxes do not grow as much as boys' voice boxes. We guys are just lucky, I guess.

Hair? Where? Hair...There?

Here's another clue you may be in puberty. You may notice hair in new places. Are you ready? You gotta be ready, 'cuz now I'm gonna talk about...some...(shhhh...)

private parts.

The first place you may notice new hair is... above your penis (pronounced **pee**-niss). I TOLD you I was going to talk about... **private parts.** This new hair above your penis is called pubic (pronounced **pyoo**-bik) hair. You will quickly notice that your pubic hair is NOT the same color as the hair on your head. Funny how Mother Nature works.

The next places you may notice new hair are: under your arms (yeah, in your PITS), on your face, on your upper lip and (later) on your chest.

It's a wild ride, dude. And you're not even driving.

I have a question for you.

Do you drive?

Do you wish you could drive?

While you might be wishing and waiting, **your hormones** (pronounced hohr-**mones**) ARE DRIVING YOU.

Who's In Charge Here, Anyway?

Ever feel like everyone's in charge, except *you*? Yeah, me too. Your parents are in charge. Your teachers are in charge. And guess what? When you are in puberty, you will feel like YOUR HORMONES are in charge!

What are hormones, anyway?

Everybody's got hormones...these invisible substances, inside our bodies. There are different kinds of hormones. One of the most famous is adrenaline (pronounced ah-**dren**-ah-lin). Adrenaline gets you pumped up when you are about to do something cool, exciting, or even scary...like playing in a big game, going out on stage, giving a speech. Have you ever felt your heart beating fast or had those "butterflies in your stomach?" That's adrenaline.

So much for the Basic Introduction to Hormones Test.

Let's move on to the really sweet hormone: testosterone (pronounced tes-**tahs**-tuh-rone).

Your body produces a ton of testosterone during puberty and adolescence. Just like adrenaline gets your body ready for a big game, a performance, or a speech, testosterone gets you ready for: **growing up**. It's what drives you to grow from a boy into a teenager into a man.

Some people even say that...

...teenagers are ruled by their "raging hormones."

I personally take a little offense to that.

But what it means is that hormones drive many of the **physical** and **emotional** changes (as in your mood, dude) that you experience in puberty and adolescence. You may wonder what is going on. One minute, everything is cool—you're growing, your voice is getting lower, you're feelin' awesome. **AND THE NEXT MINUTE**, your voice sounds like a little kid, you're not feelin' so awesome, and—your day just...tanks. Why? Because of those raging hormones.

We can thank those raging hormones for a number of things... like...

Pimples, Dimples and Zits

You are probably wondering why I threw in dimples. I wanted to see if you were still awake. Still awake? Good. Pimples, dimples and zits all have something to do with your face. Dimples on your face can be cute (when you're five). Pimples (also known as zits) are your body's reaction to all the changes going on inside you. Remember those hormones? They can make oil in your skin. Then, to complicate things, you also have these sebaceous (pronounced suh-**bay**-shuhs) glands that produce oil in your skin. These glands actually keep your skin from drying up. (Yeah, really, from drying up.)

Chill out for a minute and pause. Are you paused?
Good.
Let's give these sebaceous glands some respect.

Just picture a raisin. Got the raisin in your mind? Now, think about your skin being like the skin of a grape. Without sebaceous glands—and the oil they produce in your skin—your skin would look like a raisin. Okay, you get it. These sebaceous glands are good for your skin and keep it from drying up. But *sometimes* these sebaceous glands go a little crazy and produce more oil than your skin needs.

And *sometimes*, the oil can get stuck in your pores (the tiny holes in your skin). When the oil gets stuck in your pores, it may cause a zit.

REAL DEAL ACTION CHALLENGE #4

1) Put down your book.
2) Go to a mirror.
3) Look at those little pores in your skin.

So, maybe the oil gets stuck in one of your pores and causes a zit—maybe it doesn't. If it gets stuck in one of your pores— voila! You're the proud owner of a zit. If it doesn't get stuck in a pore, count yourself lucky. You escaped a zit. (Just a little side note: If your pores stay clean, you will be less likely to... encounter...a ZIT.)

Zits are different for everyone. Some people get none, some people get a few, and some people get a lot. Some people are more prone to getting zits, just because of the way their bodies are made up. There are soaps, ointments, and medicines to control your zits. If your zits bug you, talk to your mom, dad or trusted adult about ointments or even going to a dermatologist who can treat your skin. Hang tight. We're not done. There are things you can do to manage zits:

⇨ Wash your face in the morning and before you go to bed.

⇨ Eat on the **healthier side** (take your pick of some fruits and veggies).

⇨ Don't have too much soda and junk food (a.k.a. chips, candy, and all that).

⇨ Water helps too. As in drinking it.

⇨ One more thing. Don't pick 'em. Don't pick your nose and don't pick your zits. Enough said.

And Now For The Sen-si-tive Stuff... The Anatomy (pronounced ah-naah-tuh-me) Lesson

There is another more important thing I have to tell you about. Another sign you're in puberty. Are you ready?

It's your genitals (pronounced **jehn**-ih-tuhls). Those really **private parts**. And when they get bigger, you know YOU ARE IN PUBERTY.

Read on for the basic anatomy lesson.

First, there is your penis (see my fine illustration below). I'm guessin' you know about that. Your family might call it by its name—penis—or your family might call it something else. But...we won't go there.

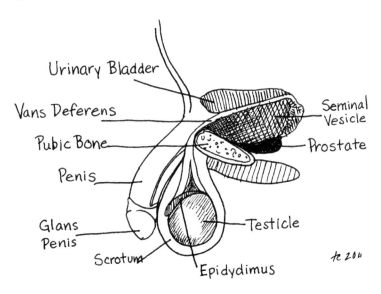

Urinary Bladder

Vans Deferens

Pubic Bone

Penis

Glans Penis

Scrotum

Seminal Vesicle

Prostate

Testicle

Epidydimus

te 2011

Under your penis, you have a bag of skin called your scrotum (pronounced **skroh**-tuhm). Some people call this "your sack," and it has a job. It holds your testicles (pronounced test-uh-**cuhls**). Sometimes you hear people refer to testicles as "balls." Heard that before? Yep, they call 'em balls. Those testicles (the balls) start to get bigger as you go through puberty. And, the skin on your scrotum ("the sack" that holds your testicles) gets darker.

Here's a piece of REAL DEAL information about your testicles (your balls). You have two. (Just kidding, you already knew that.) Your balls are actually glands that produce testosterone (that wild hormone that causes all the changes in puberty).

Did ya catch all that? Another way you know YOU ARE IN PUBERTY, is that your penis, your testicles, and your scrotum get bigger.

When you get into puberty and adolescence, you might notice that your penis takes on different forms. You'll probably notice that it is usually flaccid (pronounced **flah**-sihd). This is not to be confused with flatulence (pronounced **flat**-choo-lense), which is a fancy word for...FARTING.

We are not talking about farting.

Flaccid means that your penis is relaxed and hangs down (like usual). Another way your penis can be is erect. It stands up and it stands out—right out of your body. When a penis is erect, it gets stiff and it gets bigger. This is called an erection (otherwise known as a "hard on" by some guys). Guess what? Baby boys get erections. Believe it. I'm serious. I wouldn't joke about something like this. You probably had one when you were a baby. You were just too busy blowing bubbles and zooming cars to notice.

Are you ready for this?

It is not out of the ordinary to wake up with AN ERECTION.

Sometimes erections happen for no reason at all. The text books call those *involuntary* erections. Basically this means that you have a brain, but your penis does not. It (your penis) just rises up and gets erect, without you wanting it to. Other times it might happen because of something you are thinking about. And, maybe that something you are thinking about gets you excited. Then, some of your blood rushes to your penis. So, you get an erection from blood going to your penis. You might think this sounds a little embarrassing. But remember it is only a big deal if you make it a big deal. Probably nobody else will even notice.

Here's a tip for you.
If this happens, don't panic.
I said, don't panic.

Just think about something else. Something boring. Like homework. And your penis will calm down. Your erection will go away.

Here's another tip while we're on the subject. This came from my cousin (his name is Gabe). He told me if I was ever really concerned about this happening or if I felt self-conscious about the whole thing, I could carry a sweatshirt with me. That way, whenever my penis decided to act like a tree branch, I could casually hold my sweatshirt in front of me, or put it on my lap, and then I would be sure nobody would notice. I haven't really gone that route, but I throw it out as a good suggestion. Those second cousins on your mother's side can be pretty helpful.

Dreaming At Night—In a Swimming Pool?

Now is when I introduce you to another wild thing about puberty: wet dreams. Have you heard of them?

Like most kids, you've probably had scary dreams. You've probably had funny dreams. You've probably had dreams that make no sense (like the lion that jumped through my window last night).

Now comes the time for...wet dreams. These are the kind that happen only after you begin puberty.

So, if you are wondering if you are in puberty...and you have a wet dream...BINGO! You're there, dude.

The text book term for wet dreams is *nocturnal emission*. Let's break this down. You probably know nocturnal means night—as in the nocturnal animals that go out at night—like raccoons, skunks, naked mole rats.

So, you got the nocturnal part—at night. Now the emission part—like in a car. Emissions are what *comes out of* a car's exhaust pipe when it is running—like nitrogen gas, carbon dioxide, and water vapor.[2]

Let's put it together. A nocturnal emission is something coming out at night—BINGO! You got it, smart one. That is a wet dream.

I KNOW.
YOU'RE STILL CONFUSED.

Hang tight. I'll explain. 'Cause this is an important one. If you have a wet dream, a sticky liquid comes out of your penis while you are asleep. The sticky liquid is called semen (pronounced **see**-mihn) and it is stored in your testicles (those balls of yours). Wild, dude, huh? Hold on tight. There's more.

You may remember the dream, or maybe you will just notice a wet spot on your pajamas or on your sheets.

This is another NORMAL part of boys' development.

I know...this puberty thing is a lit-tle creep-y. Guess what? These wet dreams will slow down or stop as you get older.

....
2   http://auto.howstuffworks.com

The thought of this makes some guys embarrassed. I get that. It seems gross. Might even seem uncomfortable and a little unbelievable. But it's another one of those **normal** things.

Talking to somebody about it helps. Makes it a little more **normal**. And here's a tip. You can make up a code word (between you, mom, or dad, or that other person who helps take care of you). Some cool code that silently says: I had one of those. Time to change the sheets.

Then, you decide what makes sense for you: wash the sheets yourself, ask someone to help you, or ask someone to wash them for you (like if you're in a big rush for school, followed by soccer practice, and then a meeting, with no time-whatsoever-to-get-those-darn-sheets-in-the-washer). The code will make it more **normal** and you won't have to announce to the world (or at least anyone within hearing distance) that you **had a nocturnal emission.**

In Summary
(Because It's Always Good To Summarize)

I threw a lot at you. I gave you many clues to know when YOU ARE IN PUBERTY.

Let's review.
Just because.
It's good to review.

SIGNS OF PUBERTY

If you notice that:

your private parts get bigger

your pubic hair appears

your voice gets lower

you have a wet dream

you get hair in new places

you get some zits

YOU ARE IN PUBERTY.

MAYBE THIS WILL HELP.

Your testicles grow bigger and your scrotum gets darker.	Between ages 10 to 13
Pubic hair grows.	Between ages 10 to 15
Your body grows taller, stronger and more massive.	Between ages 10½ to 16
Your penis gets bigger.	Between ages 11 to 14½
Your voice becomes lower and deeper.	Between ages 11 to 14½
You may have wet dreams.	Between ages 11 to 17
Hair begins to grow under your arms and on your face.	Between ages 12 to 17
Pimples may appear more readily.	Between ages 12 to 17

(Taken from The Complete and Authoritative Guide: Caring for Your Teenager, The American Academy of Pediatrics.)

This might sound overwhelming. Maybe a bit confusing. Which brings me back to some of my original tips. Talk about it. Share the book. (Or just leave it lying around...and wait to see who picks it up.)

CHAPTER 2

SNIFF...SNIFF...SNIFF... AND OTHER WAYS TO KEEP YOUR FRIENDS

When puberty takes hold of you, your body takes on new—shall we say—scents? More adult smells, that is. Like sweat and the all-important, famous: Body Odor (otherwise known as **B.O.**).

This is because your body starts producing sweat glands—just like adults. And your body starts producing new smells—just like adults. Which leads me to:

SHOWERING

I realize this is not a new concept to you.

But what might be new is this. There will be a time (very soon...if not already) that you will need to take a shower pretty much every day.

Because...even though you don't think you are "dirty," you just **might smell**. You just might smell because of those adult-like sweat glands that produce sweat and B.O. (that body odor thing). These sweat glands can produce sweat and we don't even know it. But we can smell it. If **you** don't smell it, trust me that other people may smell it. Here's a tip, just for free: If you notice that you sweat at any point during the day, hop in the shower, dude. (Unless, of course, you prefer bubble baths. Knock yourself out.) 'Cuz if not, you will stink.

Another important way to manage your stink factor is:

DEODORANT

If you don't already use deodorant, think about talking to mom or dad or your trusted adult to get you some. There are lots of shapes, colors, sizes and scents to choose from. Guess what? You might like it. You might like the way it makes you smell. You'll find there are a lot of choices out there. One of the first choices is whether you use deodorant or deodorant with anti-perspirant.

Deodorant will keep you from smelling bad. Deodorant with anti-perspirant will stop you from sweating, and will also keep you from smelling bad. Some people think that anti-perspirant is not as healthy for you since it stops you from sweating. That is something for you and your trusted adult to figure out.

In the meantime, here are Bork's Ever So Helpful Tips On Deodorant:

- 👍 Use it. Every day.

- 👍 Try different ones. There are sprays and sticks, all with different scents.

- 👍 If you get a rash, try one without aluminum (on the label, dude).

The combination of the daily-shower-and-application-of-deodorant (among other things), is known as

Daily Hygiene
(Like brushing your teeth).
Taking care of it is an important step
in growing up.

I say that daily hygiene is an important step because I am arming you with something to make you comfortable and confident. Without these **daily** hygiene protocols, you may find yourself:

Standing alone...while everyone...slowly...inches...away from you, or earning a nickname

something like

smelly felly

stinky hinky

or the simple yet constant label of: U Stink.

These nicknames could actually stick with you until you're 27.

Let me throw out something else.

THINK ABOUT THIS:

Kid A does not shower or use deodorant on a regular basis, and walks by.

Kids B, C, D, along with Adults Z and M hold their breath. They actually hold their breath because Kid A **smells**, and it is just...well...**dis-gusting**.

Happens a lot.

Don't be Kid A. There's a much better way.

Shower, Use Deodorant, and Remember... Your Feet

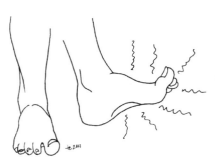

If your mom or dad is walking around, saying "WHAT is that SMELL?", it just might be your feet. Yes, dude, YOUR FEET. Put your nose to your toes. Get as close as you can. Even if you're not flexible, take a sniff. How do your feet smell?

Feet sweat. And when feet sweat, the sweat produces bacteria. And, bacteria grow in places that are damp and dark. Like where? Inside your socks and shoes.

The feet of teenage boys (like it or not) can be the stinkiest of all. King of Stink, really. But seriously, here's a golden nugget that will make your life a whole lot more pleasant: Wash your feet. Here's another tip: Wash them with a little more energy. Ready for this? Wash in between your toes. You got it. In between your toes. That's where bacteria can get stuck. And stuck bacteria stinks. I, personally, have learned that it is helpful to wash your feet every day, even if, by chance, you don't shower that day. Just remember:

Sweat = Bacteria + Dark, Damp Place = Stink

Here's another foot tip (even if you don't want one). Dry your feet after you wash them and change your socks every day. I repeat: Don't Wear Socks Two Days In A Row. When you wear socks two days in a row, you are sending a grand invitation for:

THE ITCH OF THE CENTURY

Trust me. I had it. I had The Itch of the Century and it wasn't fun.

What if, just what if, you follow Bork's tips and you still get The Itch? It might happen. If it does, you will know that it is probably

ATHLETE'S FOOT

About 70% of people get athlete's foot at some time in their lives.[3] I have no idea why it is called athlete's foot because all people—not just athletes—get it. Piano players get it. Even moms get it. If your feet suddenly feel itchy and you notice some extra dry skin around your toes and on the bottom of your feet, or you feel like there's a pin poking your toe or your foot, it's probably athlete's foot. Fear not, man. There is a cream or spray for that. Just around the corner at your local store. With the cream or spray, your athlete's foot will go away quickly. And you can go back to being a happy, itch-free dude again.

3   Dunham, Kelli. The Boy's Body Book. Kennebunkport, ME: Applesauce Press, 2007.

JOCK ITCH

Speaking of itch-free, another common *thing* that teenage boys and men can get is jock itch. It is typically more common with athletes who wear jock straps (or "cups"). (A jock strap, in case you don't know, is something to wear under clothes to protect males' private parts during athletic activities. It's also called an athletic support or a cup.) This jock itch can occur because Sweat = Bacteria + Damp, Dark Place = Stink and Itchiness. Teenage boys and men sometimes get jock itch because the sweat around their groin area can produce bacteria, which can turn into a fungus (called jock itch). Fear not, again. There is cream for this too. Just around the corner at the store.

BEFORE WE MOVE ON, I LEAVE YOU WITH ONE LAST TIP:
CLEAN IS COOL.

Which leads me to . . .

THE-NON-SCIENTIFIC-BUT-PROVEN-EVERY-DAY "LOOK 'N SNIFF TEST"

Every time you change your clothes, it is time to do the ultimate and very regular sniff test. You may have seen it done. But, to make sure you understand all the critical steps, here it is:

1. Take off your shirt.

2. Look closely at the front of it, the top of it, the bottom of it, the back of it --- and the sleeves. Inspect for any signs of dirt. Dirt is a loosely used term for any mud, pizza, chocolate, pencil, pen mark, etc., etc., which may have found a temporary home on your shirt.

3. See any leftover signs of anything you did that day? Put the shirt in the laundry.

4. Don't see any leftover signs of what you did that day? Then, assume your shirt is clean, and you can wear it again.

WRONG!
YOU ARE NOT DONE YET.

This is where the Non-Scientific-But-Proven-Every-Day "Sniff Test" comes in. Guess what? Moms and girls do it too.

5. Smell it. Yes, I said smell it. Open up that nose and take it all in. Does it smell good? Fresh? Still smell clean?

GOOD
YOU ARE NOT DONE YET.

6. Turn that thing inside out and stick that nose of yours into the armpits. Yes, I said the armpits of your shirt. Does it smell good? Fresh? Still smell clean? If your scientific conclusion, is "Ew!" that is your immediate clue to put your shirt in the laundry.

7. You're not done yet, dude. Now, check out your pants. Look clean? Smell clean? Put those pants through the Look 'n Sniff Test.

8. If you find that either your shirt or your pants are actually clean, you know what to do:

Roll them in a ball.
Chuck them in the corner.

WRONG!

If your clothes pass the Look 'n Sniff Test, put them away. Resist the temptation of putting CLEAN clothes in the laundry. This has MAJOR (and not so good) implications. This creates tons of laundry for your mom or your dad or someone else (which, by the way, makes for an unhappy mom or dad or someone else). AND, washing *clean* clothes wastes water and energy and does not **protect** the great Mother Earth on which we live. It's the only earth we have, so do your part to conserve it.

YOU ARE NOW A CERTIFIED-NON-SCIENTIFIC-BUT-PROVEN-EVERY-DAY-SNIFFER.

**Congratulations.
This is yet another important step in growing up.
Along with...**

Shaving

When many guys start to notice facial hair (that's hair on the face, man), they decide they want to shave it.

Here are some things to know about shaving:

- 👍 When you first start to shave, you may only need to shave every few days because your hair might not grow that quickly. At some point, you will probably need to shave every day. After awhile, it gets easy, just like brushing your teeth.

- 👍 It's best to shave in the direction that your hair grows. This is called "going with the grain."

REAL DEAL ACTION CHALLENGE #5

- Figure Out Which Direction You Should Shave (Going With The Grain)
- Try it.
- All you need is your face and your hand.
- Take your hand and put it next to your eye.
- Slide your hand down the side of your face, toward your chin.
- Does your hair go smoothly, under your hand?
- Good.
- That is the direction you should shave.
  That is going with the grain.

Let's Try Something Else. Just to Be Sure. It's Good to Be Sure.

- Take your hand.
- Put it on the side of your chin.
- Slide your hand up the side of your face, toward your head.
- That is NOT the direction you should shave.
- That is NOT going with the grain.

If you can't feel any hair yet (don't worry, you will, soon enough), ask your dad (or that trusted adult of yours) if you can try the **Real Deal Action Challenge #5** on him.

Guess what?

Shaving against the grain can cause soreness, redness, a rash, or bumps on your face. And, dude, who needs that? You got enough going on.

There are different kinds of razors to choose from:

A Disposable razor is a razor that you use a few times and then throw away.
A Permanent razor is a razor that has a permanent handle (one that you keep, and don't throw away) and comes with disposable blades that you use a few times and then throw away.

These razors have different numbers of blades. One that has "double blades" or "triple blades" will shave your hair a bit more closely, and give you what people call "a close shave" or "a clean shave."

With a disposable razor, you throw away the razor whenever the blade seems to be getting dull (and not shaving your hair as well). With a permanent razor, you keep the razor, and change the blade. And, you use both razors with shaving cream and after-shave lotion. This makes up your so-called "shaving kit," dude.

Another type of razor is an:

Electric razor which typically includes a rechargeable battery and power cord.

The best way to learn about shaving is to ask your dad, an older male family member, or a trusted adult. He can show you how to shave and explain what works best, so it is easy and comfortable for you.

Together, you and your so-called shaving consultant (that's your dad, uncle, brother or other male adult) can decide on the best type of razor for you, how often you should shave, the best way to do it, and the "accessories" (such as shaving cream and after-shave lotion) that you should use.

REAL DEAL ACTION CHALLENGE #6

Find your dad...or your older brother...
or your uncle...or your grandfather...
or other male adult... and...
1) Watch him shave.
2) Ask if he can show you how to shave.

CAUTION! BEWARE.

DO NOT TRY TO SHAVE
THE FIRST TIME BY YOURSELF!

RAZORS CAN REALLY CUT YOU IF
YOU DO NOT USE THEM THE RIGHT WAY!

SHAVING IS BEST DONE WITH
AN EXPERIENCED ADULT,

ALONG WITH A CHOICE OF
SHAVING CREAM OR GEL.

NEVER GLIDE THE RAZOR SIDEWAYS
OR BACKWARDS ON YOUR FACE.

IT WILL CUT YOU!

Got it?
Good.

CHAPTER 3
EVERYTHING ELSE YOU NEED TO KNOW (BUT DIDN'T REALIZE)

Look at...Who?
Me?

Can I...Look...
At You?

Remember when you were two years old? Maybe you don't. Maybe you do. You were probably like most two year olds... running, jumping, climbing, and exclaiming, "Look at me! Look what I'm doing!"

Now, not so much. You may hope that **nobody** notices you. Or maybe you hope that people **do** notice you. Everyone is different. Everyone reacts to puberty in a different way. Some people are excited about it. Some people dread it. And some people don't think it's a big deal at all.

Have you ever compared yourself to someone else? I have. A lot of other people have too. Friends do it all the time:

How tall are you?

Whadya get on that math test?

How many goals did you score?

Did ya finish that project yet?

Who's faster? Me or you? (That's more like one of those **silent comparisons**.)

Here's a time when I compared myself to one of my friends. I was in the locker room at school and all the boys were getting dressed into their P.E. uniforms. I looked at my friend and couldn't help notice that his penis looked totally different than mine. I mean TOTALLY different. Now I know why. It was because I was circumcised (pronounced **sir**-cum-sized), and he was not.

Now you are probably totally confused. Or totally curious. Or you totally don't care. If you are curious or confused, read on. If you don't care, skip to the next paragraph and I'll catch you there. On with the circumcision lesson. Some boys are circumcised when they are babies. What this means is that a doctor removes the baby boy's foreskin from his penis, often a few days after he is born. Sounds like it totally hurts, yah? It doesn't. If you ever see a friend's penis that looks different from yours, it might be because one of you was circumcised and one of you was not. If a boy's penis was not circumcised, he has a layer of skin (called foreskin) covering his penis. If a boy's penis was circumcised, he does not have a layer of skin (called foreskin) over his penis. Here's a visual, in case you want it.

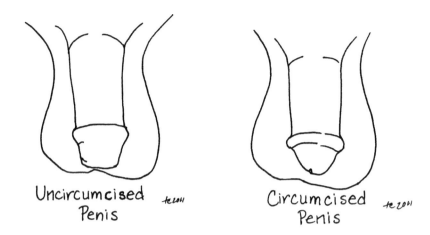

Uncircumcised Penis

Circumcised Penis

Speaking of comparisons, once I was at the doctor's office for one of those "check-ups," and I heard the doctor telling a mom that some boys wonder if their penis is too small. I heard the doctor say that pretty much never happens. Guys might talk about it...compare themselves...even joke about the size of it, but the doc pretty much said that nobody's penis is (and I quote) "too small." So, joke about it, talk about it, if you want (lots of guys do). But know that nobody's is **too small**.

The doctor also said that some boys get little bumps around their penises. They are called penile pink papules. (Try saying that five times fast.) And, about one in three boys get them. They mean nothing and are totally harmless.

Just a little tip from Bork in case you look around—and happen to embark upon a normal, schnormal comparison. What ever kind of penis you have, it will still work the same. One is not better than the other. Big, little. Long, short. Circumcised, uncircumcised. They all work the same.

Help! Am I Turning Into...A...Girl?!

Now I really got your attention.

Some boys—in the middle of puberty—have swelling under the nipples on their chest. If this happens to you, chillax. You are NOT turning into a girl. This is (once again) NORMAL. And this is (once again) a reaction to the increased hormones in your body. Even though about 3 out of 4 boys will get some growth in their breasts, it will not even be noticeable to anyone. This sometimes happens during puberty because some boys' bodies convert some of their testosterone into...estrogen...the female hormone. I told you puberty can be a wild ride. You might even feel like...

You're On A Roller Coaster

Do you remember when you were a toddler? Maybe not. Play along with me anyway.

I don't know about you, but when I was a toddler, I loved playgrounds. I loved swings.

**Up...down...up...down...
up...down.
I think you get it.**

Have you ever been on a roller coaster? Did ya like it? Up and down...up and down...and your stomach goes ooooooooooooh. That's a little bit how puberty can be. One minute you're feeling that everything is A-okay. Then, before you know it, you might feel sad or mad or excited or confused. Some adults call this being **moody**.

I remember when my dad asked me, "Why are you so... MOODY?" I quickly responded, "Dude, I'm SUPPOSED to be moody, I'm in puberty." (Well, I didn't exactly call him DUDE. I tried that once before and it didn't go over so well.)

Fact of life: adolescents and teenagers can be moody. It's because of those hormones. Remember when I told you about hormones? And how much they control what is going on in your body during puberty? Well, those mighty sweet hormones also control much of what is going on in your head and in your emotions (otherwise known as your feelings, dude).

Feeling moody, sometimes, is normal. Normal, schnormal. But I'll give you a tip: you can **feel** moody, but try not to **act** moody. Trust me on this one. It's a good tip.

Whenever you feel like snapping back at your mom or your sister or your dad or your brother, Think Twice. And zip your mouth. For just a second. Zip it for a second and then find something decent (as in appropriate) to say. You might feel moody, but don't act it. Your days will be much better that way.

Now, I'm not telling you to zip your mouth and not talk to *any-body*. Don't give everybody the silent treatment, just because you're in a puberty mood. Just zip it at those moments when you feel like you're going to say something that might be rude, nasty, or hurtful to someone. And, remember: It's Not Always What You Say, **It's How You Say It**. Teenagers are famous for rattling off something in a bad tone of voice. Trust me. Zip It and Think Twice. Pull yourself together. Rise above those hormones and don't let them take over your mouth.

During puberty, you may feel angry or irritated or sad. And, you may feel angry or irritated or sad for no apparent reason. Yep, you just feel that way (you can thank your awesomely sweet hormones for that). In other words, you may feel like:

- ☹ If anyone (ANYONE) asks you about anything (ANYTHING) right now, you're just going to snap.

- ☹ No matter who wants to talk to you, you're just not going to talk. You just don't feel like it.

- ☹ Bummed, fella. You just feel bummed and you don't really know why. And, you just feel like being alone.

You may feel any of these things (or other things). And that is totally normal, thanks to your raging, roller coaster hormones. But remember my tip: You can FEEL moody, but try not to ACT moody. Just because your hormones are making you feel...irritated...or angry...or annoyed...or sad, doesn't mean that you have the right to treat everyone the way you feel. Rise above your irritation, your anger, and your totally annoyed body, and take the high road to treat people the way you want to be treated. It's a good move.

And, last but not least, talk to someone if you can. Especially talk to someone if you are **always** feeling sad or down. Talk to...a friend...a sibling...a cousin...mom...dad...great-aunt Bea (what do you mean you don't have a great Aunt Bea?)...another aunt...uncle...grandmother...grandfather...teacher...coach...a friend's parent. Talk to someone about how you're feeling and what you're thinking. It helps. It makes the roller coaster ride a little less jerky. And it makes your days a little more smooth.

What's that? I thought I heard you mumbling. Maybe you think people won't want to listen—especially about *that* stuff. Maybe you think it is uncomfortable to talk about *that* stuff.

Guess what? Your mom, your dad, and anyone else who takes care of you wants to hear *how you're feeling* and *what you're thinking*—especially about *this* stuff. The people who take care of you choose to take care of you because they love you. They buy food for you, cook for you, drive you places, help you with your homework, fill out all those papers from school...because they love you...and because they want the best for you. And they want to help you sort through THE REAL DEAL. Remember: **They've been there. They've done that.** They were in puberty too.

It's a little known fact that *boys* like to talk while *doing something*. You can talk whenever and wherever it feels right to you... while shooting hoops...getting ready for bed...building something...driving in the car...brushing your teeth (spit out and wipe your mouth, if you choose this route)...while doing your homework (go ahead, take a break from the homework grind).

Here's one last tip: Try not to tap them on the shoulder when they have their coffee mug in one hand, their water bottle in the other, their purse or briefcase falling off their shoulder, as they are about to go out the door. That *may* not be the *best* time to talk. But just about any other time (other than rushing out somewhere) can be a good one.

REAL DEAL ACTION CHALLENGE #7

Think about whom you want to talk to.

Go ahead. Do it. **Think about it.**

Think about when you want to talk to the person.

Go ahead. Do it. **Think about a time.**

Pipe up and ask him/her some questions or tell him/her what you think about all this puberty STUFF.

This whole emotional roller coaster ride is happening because of the increased hormones in your body. At this time in your life, your body will change so much. You will change physically (how you grow, how you look). You may change socially (how you act). You may change cognitively (how you think and what you think about). One minute you might be totally cool with all the changes. You're looking forward to growing up. The next minute you might want to play around like you did when you were younger. It's a wild ride, dude. Hold on tight, and know IT'S ALL NORMAL. Normal, schnormal, dude.

What if You Don't Like Roller Coasters?

Some of us love 'em, some of us don't. Here are some tips about what you can do on the roller coaster of puberty:

☑ Stay ahead of your hunger. Have snacks. Don't skip breakfast, lunch or dinner. Don't let yourself get too hungry. (Healthy snacks will make you feel better. But you already know that.)

☑ Get physical. (Moving your fingers on your video games doesn't count.)

☑ Go outside, ride your bike, play a sport, skateboard. I think you get it.

☑ Find a fun (should I also mention safe?) activity. Add a friend to the mix.

☑ Journal. Yep. Keep a journal. Write down stuff. Any stuff. Stuff you think. Stuff you feel. Write anything and everything that comes to your mind. And don't worry about how it sounds or looks. Some of my buds say it really helps. Plus, think of it this way. You can pick it up and read it 20 years from now, and get a real laugh. It might sound like work, but it's just a good way to get stuff off your chest.

"Pier" Pressure

You've probably heard of Peer Pressure. It's called Peer Pressure because it's when your peers (people your same age) try to talk you (or dare you) into doing something...something that maybe you don't want to do or you know is wrong—even something that can be harmful, destructive or life-changing.

I call it Pier Pressure (did ya catch the change in spelling?) because it reminds me of a scenario:

IF SOMEONE TOLD YOU TO JUMP OFF A PIER
—INTO A MUDPIT OF SWARMING, HUNGRY ALLIGATORS —
WOULD YOU DO IT?

Probably not.

What if someone tells you that you will **only** be **cool** if you

JUMP OFF A PIER
—INTO A MUDPIT OF SWARMING, HUNGRY ALLIGATORS —
WOULD YOU DO IT?

Probably not. But that is what Peer Pressure is like. It can be about your "friends" or your peers trying to talk you into doing something, just to be cool or "part of the group," even if it's doing something stupid.

Why do some kids do things they don't want to do? Why do some kids do things they know are wrong or even harmful? It's because of peer pressure. You can resist peer pressure. I know, because I've done it. And I still have a load of cool and awesome friends. And that's because a friend is somebody who will still like you and hang out with you even if you decide not to go along with what some dudes are telling you to do.

If someone (even a friend) asks you to

DO something

    SNIFF something

        SWALLOW something

       DRINK something

         SMOKE something

           TRY something

that you know or **even think** might be

HARMFUL Or

    ILLEGAL Or

        DANGEROUS Or

           NOT IN YOUR BEST INTEREST Or

         UNSAFE

Ask yourself this:
Would this make my parents proud?
Then ask yourself this:
What is the worst thing that can happen if I do this?

Answer that honestly.

Think about everything that could happen to you if you do it. Because it just might happen. And it might not be good. It could be very bad. It could be something that you regret...for a long time. Even for the rest of your life. It may even change your life. And not for the good.

And, then, remember this:

There are loads and loads and millions of kids and adults who DID NOT do the harmful or the illegal or the dangerous or the unsafe thing their peers pressured them to do. And those same loads and loads and millions of kids and adults were cool and still had tons of friends. You know why? Because TRUE friends will hang out with you even if you don't do the undesirable (and stupid) thing they (or others) want you to do.

You know what else? They just might be waiting for some-one to take a stand, to be stronger than the rest, and to do the right thing. They just might not be strong enough to do it themselves.

One more thing. If one of your "friends" decides he doesn't want to be your "friend" any more (just because you didn't do something he wanted you to do), he is not really your friend. Who needs a "friend" who gets you into trouble and leads you into bad situations? You got enough going on without having "friends" like that.

REAL DEAL ACTION CHALLENGE #8

Find an adult you like to talk to.

Ask that person about a time he or she ran into peer pressure.

You will find that **everyone** ran into **some kind** of peer pressure (And you might hear some pretty interesting stories.)

Kids (especially adolescents sometimes) do things they don't want to do. They do things that are just...basically...stupid... because of peer pressure. Kids (especially adolescents sometimes) do things just to fit in. Not to feel left out. Everybody wants to **fit in**. That's normal. Even adults want to **fit in**. The trick is to fit in with the right group. The group that does what is right. The group that thinks you're good just the way you are, doing just what you do. Not having to prove anything to anyone. It feels better hanging out with those people. It's more fun too. No worries, no stress. Just being you.

Peer pressure is real. And peer pressure is hard. But anyone can stand up to it if he really wants to. Be strong enough and big enough to make the right choice. You'll know what the right choice is. If you have any doubt, dig down deep. You'll know what to do.

Be strong.

Be cool.

Stand above "the crowd."

If you ever have any doubt about what to do, talk to someone about it. Talk to a friend, a cousin, an aunt, an uncle, mom, dad. You may think they won't understand, but they will. They really will.

CHAPTER 4
AND NOW FOR THE REALLY INTERESTING STUFF

The stuff kids wonder about. The stuff kids might talk about. The stuff you need to know. Dude, I'm talking about s-e-x. Hold on tight. Here we go.

Do you know you have a reproductive system?

Yes?

Good.

What exactly is a reproductive system?

Let's start with reproduce. To reproduce means to produce offspring—as in human KIDS. Believe it or not, some of the changes during puberty are because you can reproduce.

Whoa, wild, dude. *That* probably seems a little scary. And, it is. The last thing you can imagine right now is HAVING KIDS. But that's for another book—at another time.

Physically, after going through puberty, you have the ability to reproduce...to have offspring...just like animals and the birds and the bees. I guess way back in the old days, people had kids when they were really young, and our bodies are still made up that way. But now, people live much longer. And now, we wait *a lot longer* to have kids. We wait until we are much older, and all grown up, with a career and a marriage and all that.

Hey, by the way, speaking of the birds and the bees, did you know that *"the birds and the bees"* is a code name for...SEX... and reproducing and ALL THAT?

Yep. It is.

Remember when I told you knowledge is power?

Hold on tight for a little knowledge and a lot of power and strength.

'Cuz in a minute you will know the REAL DEAL about SEX.

You already know that the word sex can describe your gender, as in whether you are a male or a female. But the sex we are talking about is the thing that a man and a woman do together that produces a baby.

Some people use code words for sex.
Some code names you may hear are:

DOING IT
Getting it on
The Birds and the Bees

You may already know what sex is. Making Out. Kissing and **Other Stuff**. Not exactly.

The word sex is short for sexual intercourse. Another (adult) term that some people use for sex is: making love. This is because when two people have sexual intercourse and make a baby, it is a way for them to show they love each other and get as physically close as possible. When a man and a woman have sexual intercourse or make love, they can actually make a little person (well, okay a baby).

Before I go on, I think I'll warn you that what I am going to tell you might sound:

1) a bit unbelieveable
2) totally gross
3) something you never want to think about again.

Although you might find this unbelievable or totally gross, I will remind you that it is...

...totally natural.

It is so totally natural that animals do it. That's how they make those cute little puppies...kittens...baby elephants...lambs, et cetera, et cetera, et cetera.

Let's drill down to the basics.

We'll start at the beginning. That's a good place to start.

To make a baby, a man's sperm must get together with a woman's egg.

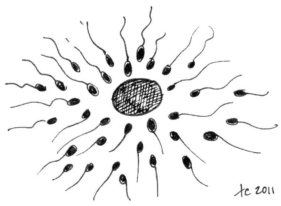

One egg.
Lots of sperm, swimming to the egg.

Here's how it works:

A man has a penis.

A woman has a vagina (rhymes with China, pronounced va-**jhine**-ah).

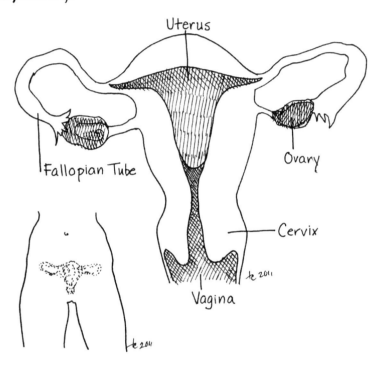

When you're older and ready to become a dad, an erect penis can actually come in handy.

HERE'S HOW:

When the man's penis is erect, he puts it into the woman's vagina.

When the man's penis enters the woman's vagina, it emits (sends out) that whitish liquid called semen (pronounced **see-mihn**) into the vagina. This semen comes out of the same hole that pee comes out of (now you're probably really freaking out). Semen is actually the same liquid that comes out of a boy's penis when he has a wet dream. When the penis emits semen, the semen carries tiny little sperm into the woman's vagina. These sperm actually look a bit like little tadpoles (only much, much, MUCH smaller). You need a microscope to see sperm. When a sperm meets up with an egg, a new cell is created that grows into a baby.

This is a fascinating system you got there in your body, huh?

The baby grows in the woman's uterus (pronounced **yoo**-tuh-ruhs) for about nine months, until it is ready to enter the world. We can't really see the woman's uterus. To us, it looks like the baby grows in the woman's stomach. But trust me, dude. The baby grows in the uterus. It's not in the mom's stomach, floating around with the pizza she ate for lunch.

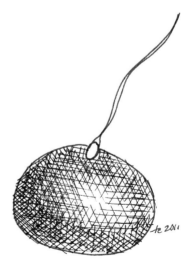

After the baby grows in the woman's uterus for about nine months, the muscles inside the woman's uterus push the baby out through the vagina. And, the baby is born. The baby actually comes out of the woman's vagina, in between her legs.

(I told you this might freak you out.) Natural, schmatural, dude, just like the horses and the dogs and the cats. It's the way Mother Nature works.

Sometimes if that is not possible, the mom has an operation called a cesarean (pronounced sah-**sayr**-eeh-uhn) (or c-section) in which the doctor makes an incision through the mom's stomach to pull out the baby safely. I know this might sound h-o-r-r-i-f-i-c, but don't worry. The doctor gives the woman anesthesia (just like you get when you have a cavity filled), so the mom and the baby don't even feel any pain. And the doctor brings the baby out into the world.

Talking about babies being born, did you ever think about the word birthday? Probably when you think about it, you think of cake and presents and parties.

Did you ever think that it is actually the celebration of your birth—day?

(That special day when you entered the world, after spending nine months in your mom's uterus?)

Now, that's a day to celebrate.

Give yourself a pat on the back.

Not only did your mom bring you into this world on your birth day, but she went through this process called "labor" to do it. Ever heard of a "woman going into labor?" That is the term that describes what happens right before the baby is born. Dude, heads up on that word, "labor." It is called labor because it is not easy. It is work (labor)! It can be hard and painful work for some moms. So, dude, remember that. (And thank your mom.)

Let me tell you (in case you don't know) how this labor and "being born" thing works. Remember what I've always told you: Knowledge is power. It makes you strong. The more you know, the better you are.

Onto the specifics of labor and birth...

A woman's body "tells" her when the baby is ready to come into the world. Her body tells her she is "going into labor" by these things called contractions. Contractions are like stomach pains. I don't mean like when you ate too much cake and drank too much soda too fast, I mean like stomach pains like you can never imagine. Sometimes labor lasts just a few hours and sometimes it can last for a whole day and night or more. These contractions come from the baby trying to make its way out. It is actually the uterus contracting and expanding, and preparing to push the baby out through the woman's vagina. The woman then pushes the baby out (which takes a lot of hard work and energy). That's why it's called...labor. Yep, that's why.

Now, put your book down and take a moment to examine your belly button. That's right. I said: Examine your belly button. Do you have an innie or an outie?

I'LL WAIT A MINUTE WHILE YOU CHECK.

Do you know why you have a belly button? That is how you got your food while you were in your mom's uterus. While you were in your mom's uterus, you got your food through your umbilical cord, which came out of your belly, and was attached to the placenta (plah-**sen**-tah) inside your mom's uterus. That's how babies eat and drink. Once the baby gets out into the real world, the baby drinks milk, so the baby doesn't need the umbilical cord. Just moments after the baby is born, the doctor clips off the umbilical cord. (Don't worry, don't scream. It doesn't hurt. It didn't hurt you or me and it doesn't hurt the little baby that is being born in the minute you are reading this.) The doctor then ties up the end of the umbilical cord and, VOILA, the baby is the proud owner of its first and only belly button.

And that, my friend, is THE REAL DEAL. Sex. Reproduction. The Birds and The Bees.

One last thing, before we wrap this all up:

CHAPTER 5

HOW TO SURF THE BIG WAVE OF PUBERTY (AND END UP ABOVE WATER)

I don't know about you, but I am very lucky to have a great-grandma who is 102 years old. No joke. For real. And, I have discovered that grandmas, great-grandmas, and even moms actually know a lot.

This is what I'm talking about:

TUDE
ATTITUDE

We all got attitude. I'm talking about the kind of attitude you need—**to surf through puberty**.

The kind that Grandma talks about.

I know, you say: Attitude, schmatitude. I don't really care.

But caring about your attitude (and the kind of attitude you have) is an important part of growing up.

You gotta care because attitude shows THE KIND OF PERSON YOU ARE. Your attitude says everything about you. Even without speaking, you show what kind of attitude you have. Do you have a positive attitude or a negative one?

⇨ Are you the kind of guy your friends want to be around?

⇨ Are you the guy that your friends' parents want around?

⇨ Or are you a grump?

⇨ Are you the kind of guy who makes it all happen— with a good attitude?

⇨ Or are you the kind who makes it all halt with a bad attitude?

⇨ Are you the kind of guy who sees the glass half full?

⇨ Or half empty?

Here is where Grandma comes in.

My grandma always says:

👍 If life gives you lemons, make lemonade. (Make the best of the situation. And always remember, whatever situation you are in, it could be worse. You can *always* imagine a worse situation if you really try.)

👍 There is always a bright side.

👍 For every minute you are angry, you lose 60 seconds of happiness.

So, take a check on your 'tude, dude. And make it a good one. No matter what else is going on around you, or within you, your attitude says everything about you.

You know what else my grandma taught me? That **sleep** is important. The amount of sleep you get impacts:

- ✓ how you grow
- ✓ how you feel
- ✓ how you look
- ✓ how you act

When you don't get the amount of sleep your body needs, you won't feel as well, look as good, and you will be grumpy and irritable (that means the littlest thing will irritate the heck out of you).

You know what else? A United States senator once told my grandpa (he's the one married to my grandma) that the two hours before midnight are the best hours of sleep for your body. Yep, between 10 pm and midnight. And remember, most teens need between 8-10 hours of sleep a night.

And one more thing before I leave you. **Laughing**. Yep, you got it. **Laughing**.

Do it. It's good. Laugh with others. Laugh by yourself. Laugh whenever you can. (Just don't laugh **at** others. That's not cool.) Little known fact: When you laugh, your body releases some totally sweet hormones called endorphins (en-**door**-fins). Endorphins make your body feel better and make you feel more happy.[4] So, if something makes you smile and laugh, go for it. Let that smile and laughter rip. It'll make you feel good. Some smart college person in the happy state of Pennsylvania

....
4   http://www.readysetgofirness.com/newsletter/39_Lovesthoseendorphins.html

actually discovered (through research and all) that laughing can increase your intelligence.[5] Cool.

And, now I leave you with this:

Bork's Quick and Easy Guide to Surviving Puberty

☑ Get enough sleep.

☑ Eat healthy.

☑ Talk.

☑ Play.

☑ Remember there are a ga-zillion people who survived it.

☑ Remember there are another ga-zillion people going through it.

(Okay. Well I didn't really research this one. But let's just say there are a lot.)

5   http://serendip.brynmawr.edu/exchange/node/2054

There you have it. Me, Bork, having revealed The Real Deal.

That is the story of life. The birds and the bees. Sex. The real deal. And everything else leading up to it.

And you are knowledgeable. You are strong and powerful, knowing the real deal about all the things your buds are talking about...or wondering...or just plain making up because they don't know any better. Maybe they want to read and learn from Bork. You don't need to tell them my whole ridiculous inherited name. You can just tell them to find Bork and The Real Deal.

(Oh, by the way, someone who read this before you wanted me to mention that girls go through puberty too. Some of the same stuff. And some different stuff. But they go through it too. Now, that's a whole other book right there.)

Resources

American Medical Association. Boy's Guide To Becoming A Teen. San Francisco, CA: Jossey-Bass, 2006.

Cole, Joanna. Asking About Sex and Growing Up. New York, NY: First Beech Tree, 1988.

Dunham, Kelli. The Boy's Body Book. Kennebunkport, ME: Applesauce Press, 2007.

Harris, Robie H. It's Not The Stork! Cambridge, MA: Candlewick Press, 2006.

Harris, Robie H. It's Perfectly Normal. Somerville, MA: Candlewick Press, 1994.

Harris, Robie H. It's So Amazing! Somerville, MA: Candlewick Press, 1999.

Mayle, Peter. "What's Happening To Me?" Secaucus, NJ: Lyle Stuart, Inc., 1975.

Mayle, Peter. "Where Did I Come From?" New York, NY: Kensington Publishing Corp., 1977.

The American Academy of Pediatrics. Caring For Your Teenager. New York, NY: Bantam Dell, 2003.

The Real Deal Index

About the Author

Terri Shearer Trenchard has a master's degree in Education and Human Development from The George Washington University. As a former teacher, manager, and organization development specialist, she currently applies her knowledge and experience in various educational, leadership, and spiritual settings with children. She lives in Ellicott City, Maryland with her husband and their two children.